TOMU OONO

PLANNING/STORY **SUNRISE**

ORIGINAL SCRIPT **MASAFUMI NISHIDA**

ORIGINAL CHARACTER AND HERO DESIGN **MASAKAZU KATSURA**

CRASH
SWISH
DIDN'T I TELL YOU THAT YOU'RE BARNABY'S FOIL?!
I CAN'T BELIEVE YOU LEFT BARNABY BEHIND!
HE SAID HE DIDN'T WANT TO USE HIS POWER.
THEN MAKE HIM USE IT!

YOU'RE HIS SENIOR, SO YOUR JOB IS TO OFFER ENCOURAGE-MENT!
YIKES
I GUESS ...
I CAN'T WORK WITH HIM.

HE'S SO NAIVE.
THINGS HAVE JUST BEGUN, BARNABY.
YOU'RE BOTH DRAWING ATTENTION AS THE FIRST SUPERHERO DUO.

YOU REVEALED YOUR IDENTITY FOR A REASON. IF YOU MISS THIS CHANCE, IT WILL ALL HAVE BEEN IN VAIN.
AM I WRONG?
...

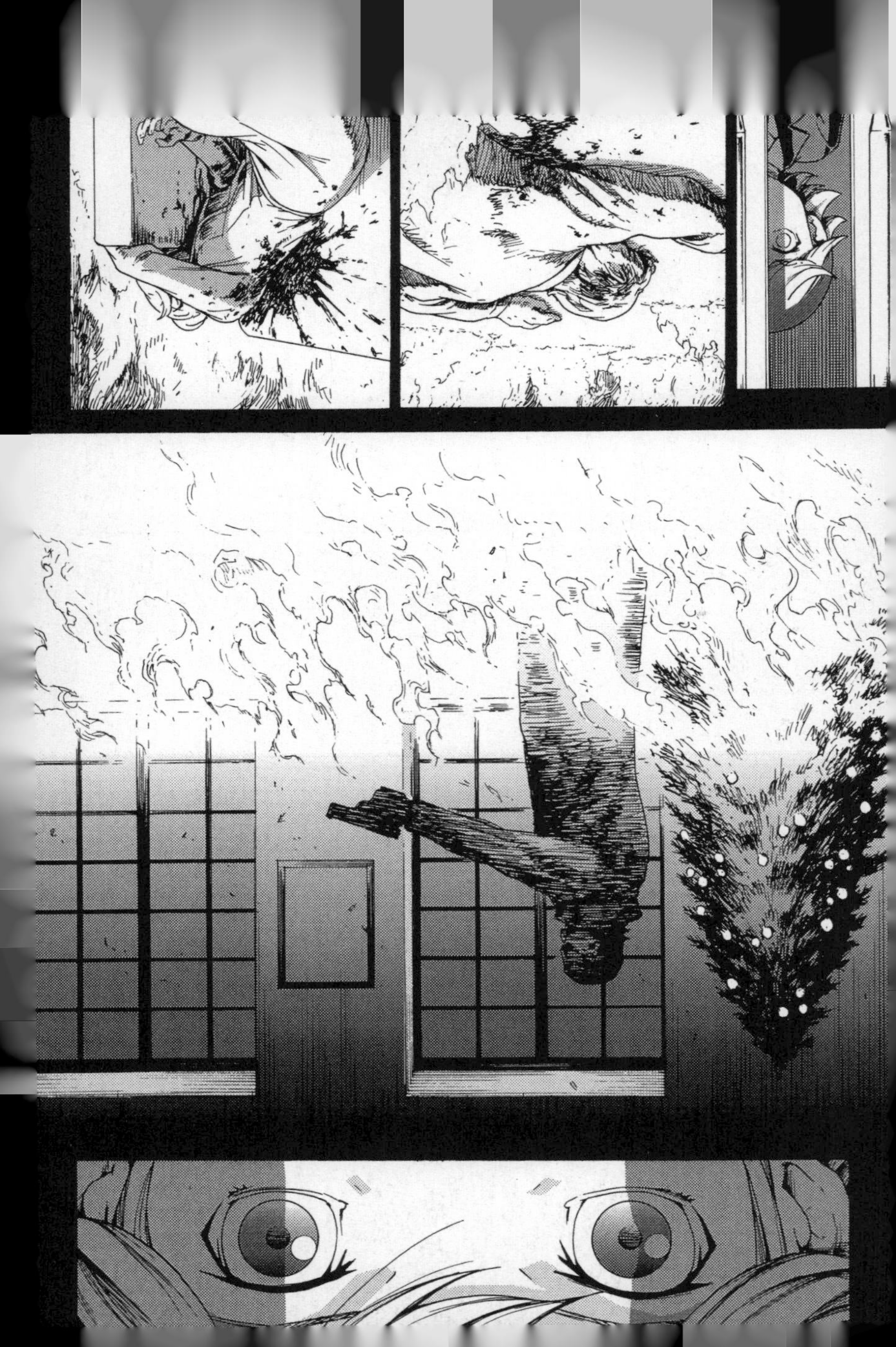

BECOMING FAMOUS WILL HELP YOU...
...TO LEARN THE TRUTH BEHIND THE MARK YOU'RE AFTER.
DON'T WORRY. SOMEDAY, YOU WILL AVENGE YOUR PARENTS.
JUST TRUST ME.
...

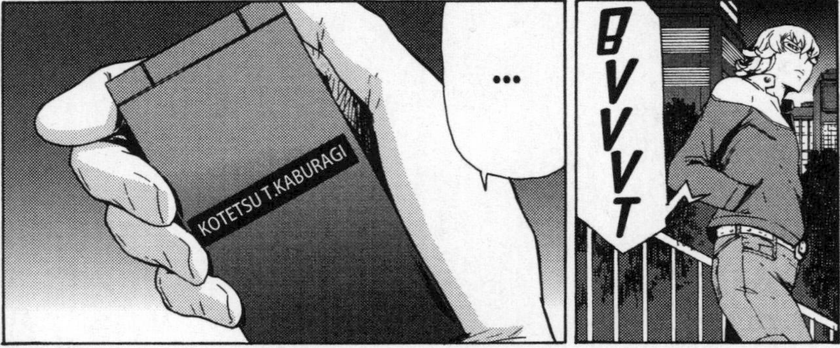

HEY! DON'T IGNORE ME!

SHF

DON'T BOTHER ME.
HUP
GEEZ!
YOU'RE ALWAYS SO UPTIGHT, LI'L BUNNY!

STOP CALLING ME THAT!
HOW 'BOUT WE GET SOME FOOD?
SORRY. I HAVE THINGS TO DO.
STOMP STOMP
H-H-HEY!

I ALREADY GOT EVERYONE TOGETHER!
?

YEAH, CHECK OUT MY BOD!

OOH ...

WHY ARE WE HAVING A WELCOMING PARTY FOR THAT ROOKIE?

WHY NOT? HE PUTS ON AIRS BUT ALSO WANTS TO GET TO KNOW US. THAT MYSTERIOUS ATMOSPHERE TURNS ME ON!

I WAS A FAILURE, BUT EVERYONE KNEW WHO *HE* WAS.
HE WAS THE FOCUS OF ATTENTION AT THE HERO ACADEMY.
MYSTERIOUS? I ACTUALLY KNOW HIM PRETTY WELL...

SORRY, GUYS!

YOU'RE LATE, KOTETSU!

I GOT ALL CLEANED UP BEFORE YOU GUYS CAME OVER!

WHY? BARNABY IS THE GUEST OF HONOR.
EXCUSE ME...
MR. WILD, WHY DON'T WE INTRODUCE OUR-SELVES?
SOUNDS GOOD.
OOH! I'LL START!
GOOD EVENING, HANDSOME!
I'M FIRE EMBLEM. MY REAL NAME IS NATHAN SEYMOUR.
I MAY NOT LOOK THE PART, BUT HELIOS ENERGY IS...
YOU'RE THE OWNER. I KNOW.
HUH?
YOU DON'T HAVE TO TELL ME. I ALREADY KNOW.
OH...
HE'S AN HONOR STUDENT! HE DOES HIS RESEARCH!
OKAY, NEXT!

I'M...
THAT'S ENOUGH.
HUH?
I ALREADY LOOKED YOU UP.

HEY! WHAT A JERK!
PSST PSST
HE'S JUST NERVOUS ABOUT MEETING EVERYONE!
I'M GOING HOME.
WHAAAT?!

THIS IS A WASTE OF TIME.
COME ON, MAN!
WHAT'S WITH THE ATTITUDE ?!
WE ONLY CAME BECAUSE YOU SAID YOU WANTED TO GET TO KNOW US!
WHAT'S YOUR PROBLEM ?!
HUH?
I NEVER SAID THAT.
YOU SAID YOU WANTED TO GET TO KNOW ME.
HUH?!
YEAH, ABOUT THAT...

KOTETSU!
I JUST THOUGHT WE'D ALL WORK TOGETHER BETTER AS FRIENDS, SO...

MNCH MNCH
SO YOU LIED?
UH...

YOU DISGUST ME.
YOU SUCK!

HOLD ON. I DON'T UNDER-STAND WHAT'S GOING ON.
I'LL EXPLAIN IT LATER.

LET'S USE THIS OPPOR-TUNITY TO BE FRIENDS!

FRIENDS?
DON'T MAKE ME LAUGH. WE'RE RIVALS.
UH...

NOW IF YOU'LL EXCUSE ME...
HEY, BUNNY!

MY SHURIKEN NEEDS CLEANING...
I NEED TO WALK JOHN.
MNCH MNCH
NO WAY!

BEEP BEEP BEEP BEEP
!
!!

BONJOUR, HEROES.
WE HAVE A SITUATION IN THE STERN MEDAILLE DISTRICT.
A ROBBER HAS STOLEN A STATUE WORTH HUNDREDS OF MILLIONS OF STERN DOLLARS!
SO GET ON IT!

WHOOSH

POOF
FWOO...

OH, NO! I'M SCARED OF THE DARK!
YOW! DON'T TOUCH ME THERE!

NOW IT'S NOT SO SCARY.
BUT NOW *YOU'RE* SCARY!

FRZZ
...

WOW ... THOSE EARRINGS WOULD STRETCH OUT MY EARS!
TUG

OH?
WANNA TRY THEM ON?
NO, NO, THAT'S OKAY!

UM...

...WHY ARE WE RUNNING ?
BECAUSE IT'S FASTER THAN WALKING!

WHY DON'T YOU JUST FLY THERE?
I CAN'T. I NEED THE JET PACK FOR SPEED.

SO THEN WITH-OUT IT...
YEP!

I ONLY FLOAT!
HA HA HA HA!
GAH
FWUF

SKY HIGH!! SKY HIGH!!
PWOOOO
HA HA HA HA!

IT'S ONE THING AFTER ANOTHER TODAY!!
UGH!
WHSH

AOLN

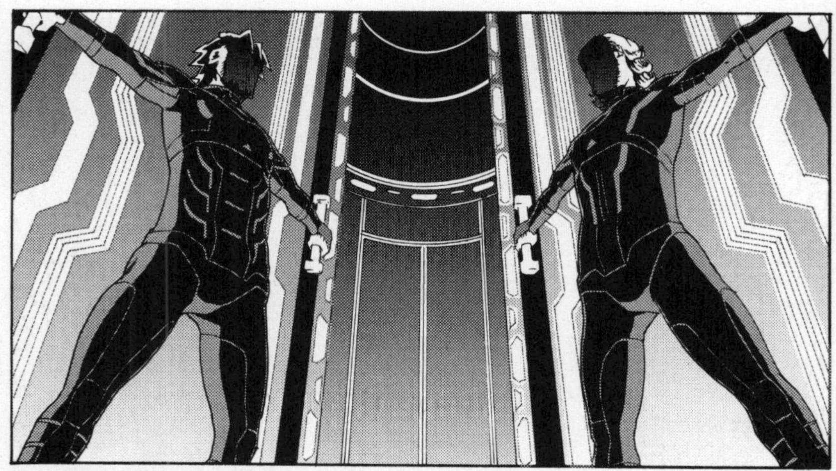

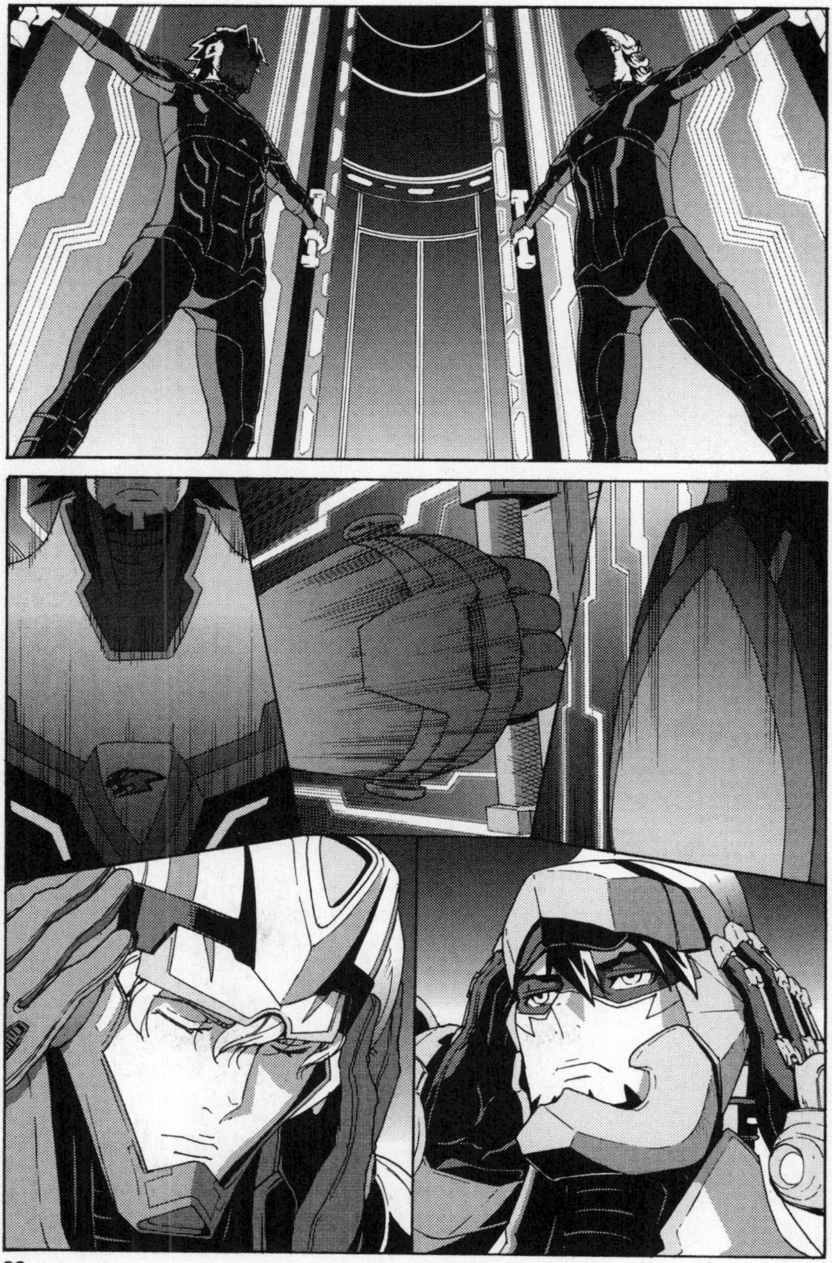

YAAAAH!!
WEEEEEE!!

THE SUSPECT IS STILL ON THE RUN WITH THE STATUE OF JUSTICE IN HIS POSSESSION!
?!
IS THAT ...?!
YES. IT'S THE SYMBOL OF PEACE THAT MR. LEGEND ONCE RETRIEVED FROM DANGEROUS CRIMINALS.
DO YOU UNDERSTAND WHAT ITS THEFT MEANS?

THE PEOPLE WILL LOSE THEIR TRUST IN HEROES!
GET IT BACK AT ALL COSTS!

AT ALL COSTS !!!

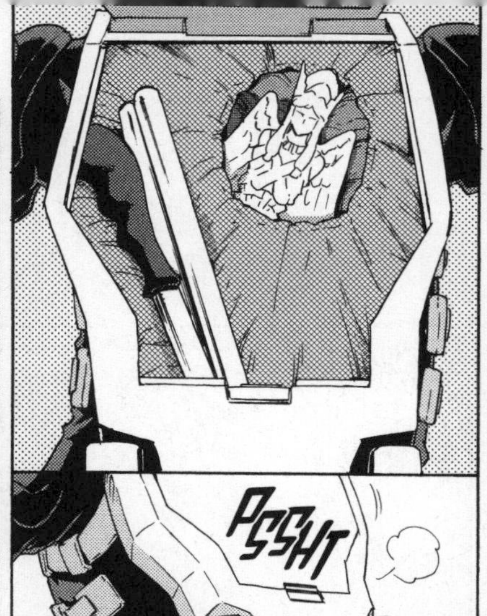

SHW
EEEE

HUP

!!

KLIK
WHAM
WOO-HOO!
SHWRRRRR
THE SUSPECT SLIPPED PAST THE POLICE!
AND YET THE HEROES ARE NOWHERE TO BE SEEN!
WHAT ARE THEY DOING ?!
THERE THEY ARE!

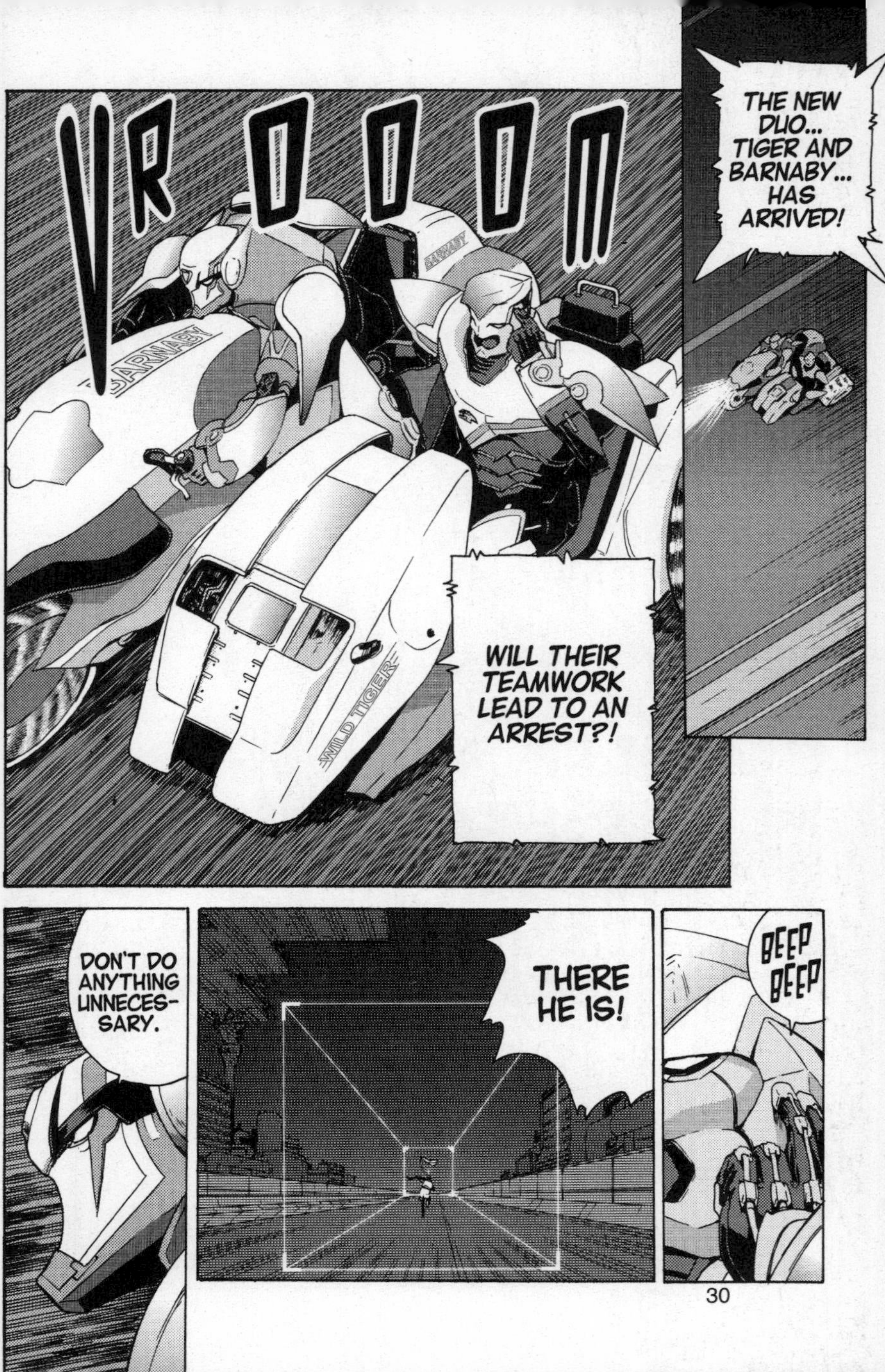

THE NEW DUO... TIGER AND BARNABY... HAS ARRIVED!

VROOOM

BARNABY

WILD TIGER

WILL THEIR TEAMWORK LEAD TO AN ARREST?!

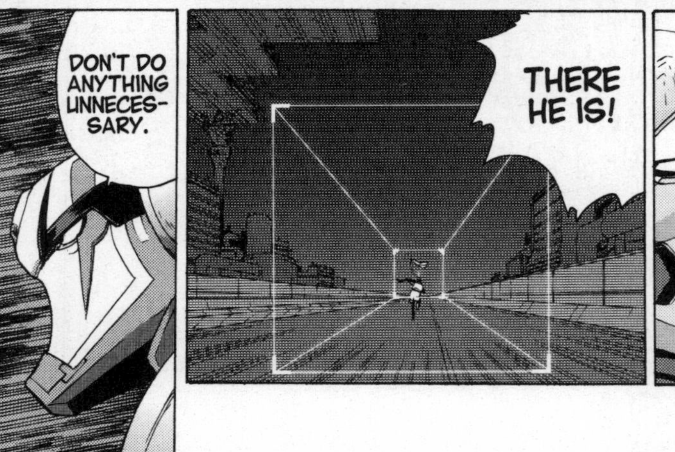

I KNOW, I KNOW. JUST GO CATCH HIM!
SHMP

GWOOSH
WHOOOA!!

THERE'S A CONSTRUCTION BARRICADE 200 METERS AHEAD.
TIME TO SPLIT UP.
HUH? WHAT?

BEEP BEEP
GYAAAH!
DANGER
KEEP OUT KEEP OU

STINK

WHOA!
VROOM
KCHIK
WHRRRR
VROOOM

VROOOSH

WHAM

OUTTA
MY
WAY!

VROOM
UH-OH!
MY
POINTS!
ZIP
HEY!

RMMM
HEH...
BLUE ROSE, BARNABY BROOKS JR. AND WILD TIGER...
!
VROOM
WHO WILL NAB THE SUSPECT FIRST?!
URGH!
VR OOM
BARNABY
YOU GUYS...
VR OOOOOOOM

THIS IS NO TIME FOR A CAR CHASE!
VROOM
VROOOOOM
SCREECH
HUH?
SCREECH

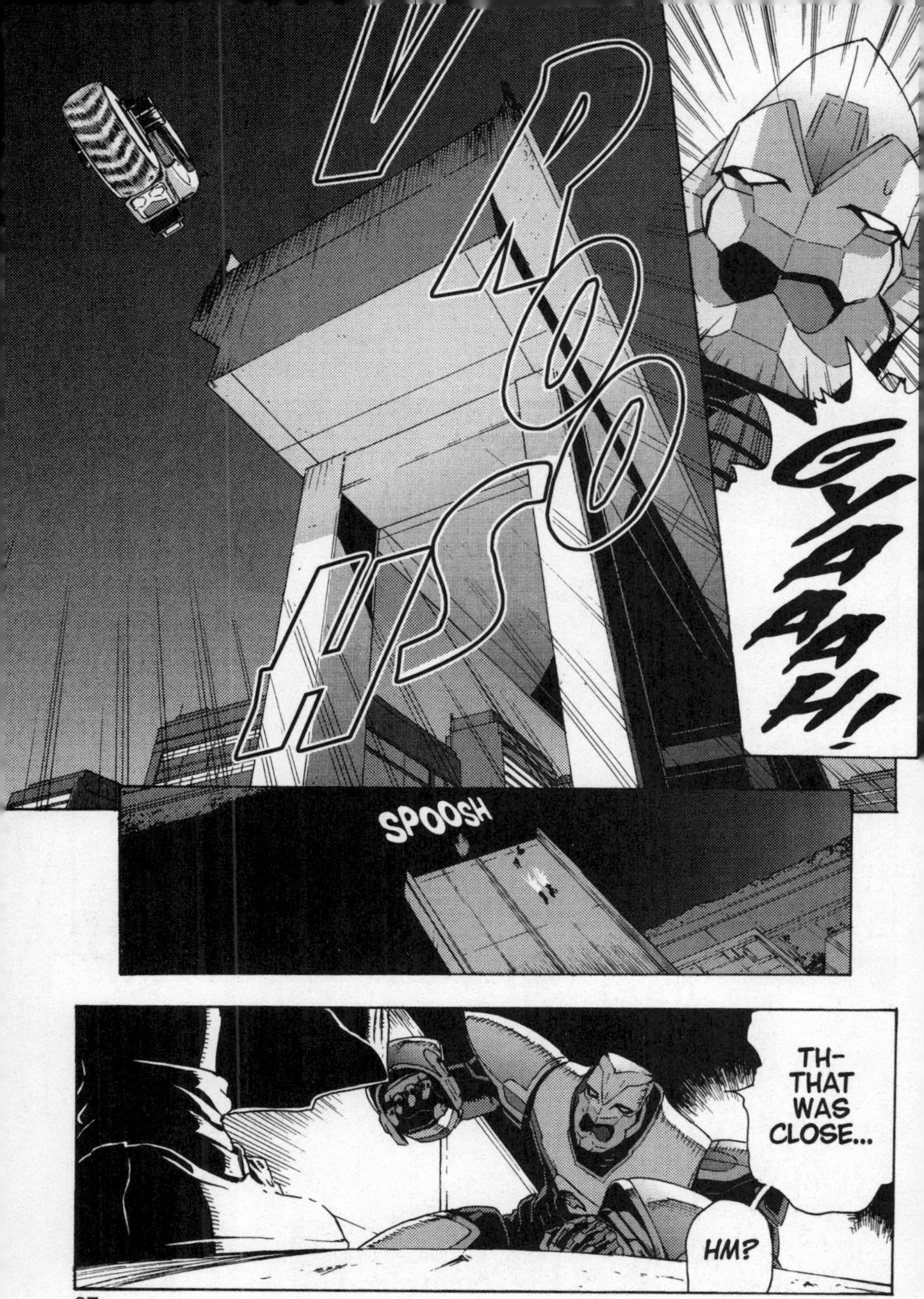

GYAAAAH!
VROOSH
SPOOSH
TH-
THAT
WAS
CLOSE...
HM?

WHAT THE?

?!

HUH?!

IT'S ALL YOUR FAULT THAT I LOST HIM!
?
?

THE SUSPECT DIS-APPEARED!
WHERE COULD HE HAVE GONE?!

SO, UH...
...WHAT'RE YOU DOING HERE, OLD LADY?

...
HEH!

TIGER & BUNNY
THE MOVIE
The Beginning

HE FLED INTO AN AMUSE-MENT PARK...

WOO-HOO!
SPROING

...
THIS NEEDS TO BE MORE EXCITING!
EEK!
WHOA!
SHWRR
SKR
HEH.
CLOMP

THE POINTS ARE MINE!!
KLANK
ROCK BISON WAS LYING IN WAIT FOR THE SUSPECT!
OH! BUT DRAGON KID IS THERE TOO!

HEH...
SWIP
HUH?!
ZAP
ZAP
ZAP
OOGAAH!
WHAT?! ROCK BISON?!!

CREEEK

OH
NO!

EEEK!
LOOOOM
THIS DOESN'T LOOK GOOD!
WAP
ROCK BISON STOPPED IT!
SLAM
COME TO ME!
HOW DID THAT HAPPEN?!
THOOM

HERE COMES SKY HIGH!
SWOOSH
HM?
SWSH
STOP RIGHT THERE!

SWIRRRL
FWSH
HIIIGH

HUH?!
WHAM
AGH!!

SWOOOSH
HMM?
YOU WON'T GET AWAY!
HIGH!
FWOOSH
SNAP
WHOOOM!
10

SHKANG

IT APPEARS THE KING OF HEROES HAS A STRONG TAIL WIND TODAY!

NOK NOK
HMM ...

HAND OVER THE STATUE OF JUSTICE!
IF YOU WANT IT THAT BADLY ...

YES!
SKRF

...COME AND TAKE IT FROM ME.
HUH?

HM?!
WOOSH
WHOA!
KRAK
UMPH!
I'M ENDING THIS LITTLE CHASE!
KRIK KRAK

ARE YOU SURE ABOUT THAT?

MY ICE IS A LITTLE COLD...

...BUT YOUR CRIME HAS BEEN PUT COMPLETELY...

YOU'RE TAKING...

...TOO MUCH TIME!
DON'T INTER-RUPT!
IF YOU'VE GOT TIME FOR THAT SPIEL...
FWSH
...JUST PUT HIM ON HOLD ALREADY!
HEY! BUTT OUT!
PSHHHH

...
FLASH

BOOM
?!!
EEEK!
EEEK!
FWOOSH
THAT'S AGAINST THE RULES!
SAME TO YOU!
WHAT JUST HAP-PENED?!
HEH!

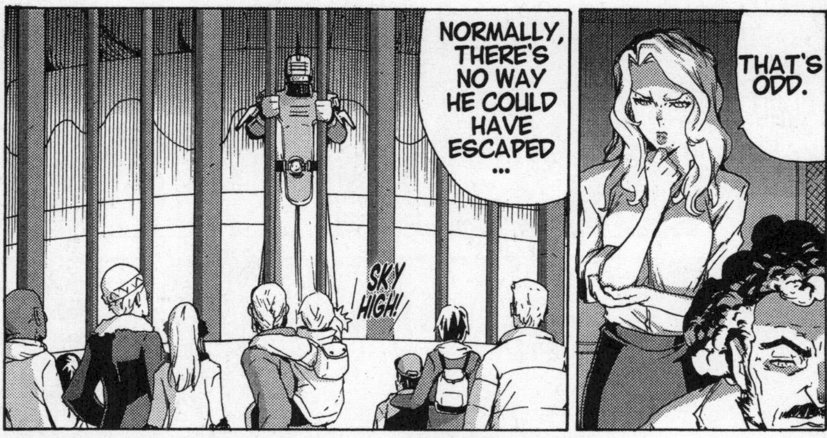
THAT'S ODD.
NORMALLY, THERE'S NO WAY HE COULD HAVE ESCAPED ...
SKY HIGH!

THE SUSPECT REMAINS ON THE RUN!

...

HEH HEH HEH...
LIVE

THERE HE IS!

KCHIK

YOU PROMISED YOU WOULDN'T DO ANY-THING RASH.
!

DID I?

YOU'RE ALWAYS SO...

THEN WHAT DO YOU PROPOSE? HE'S A SLIPPERY DEVIL!
HE MAY BE FAST, BUT HE WON'T ESCAPE IF WE BOTH CORNER HIM WITH OUR POWERS ACTIVATED.

WE TRAP HIM BETWEEN US...

JUST FOLLOW MY ORDERS.

THIS IS A GREAT OPPOR-TUNITY TO DISPLAY SOME TEAM-WORK.
I DON'T CARE HOW, LET'S JUST CATCH HIM.

BUT IT'S NOT JUST THE ROOKIE!

WHSH

STOMP

NOW!
WHSH
RAAAAAGH!
TMP TMP TMP TMP TMP TMP

WHAMMO
WHY ARE YOU...?!
I DON'T KNOW!
NOT A BAD IDEA...
CLAP CLAP
...BUT YOU WON'T CATCH ME THAT WAY!
SHWRRR

SHMP
ARGH!
HUP
!
TOMP
SKIDD
WHOA!
HRAH!
FWSH

FWASH
RAAGH!
TMP TMP TMP TMP TMP
WHAAAH?!!
WHOOPS...

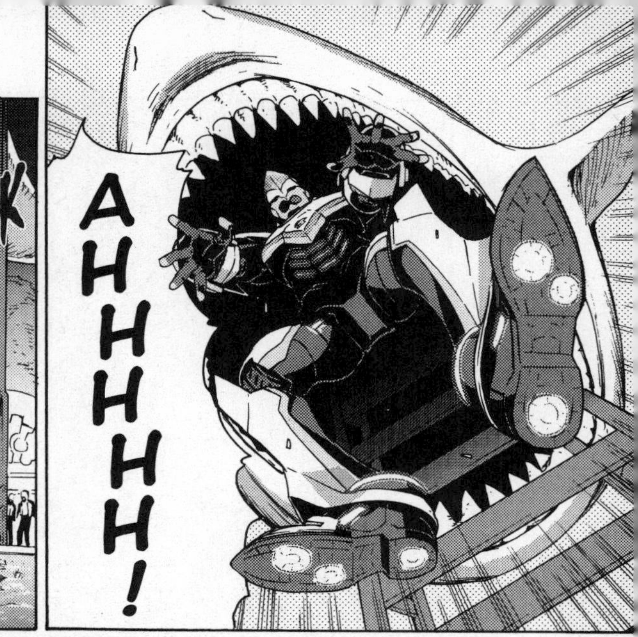
AHHHHH!

SNAP KRAK
SPLOOSH

SHWRRR
...

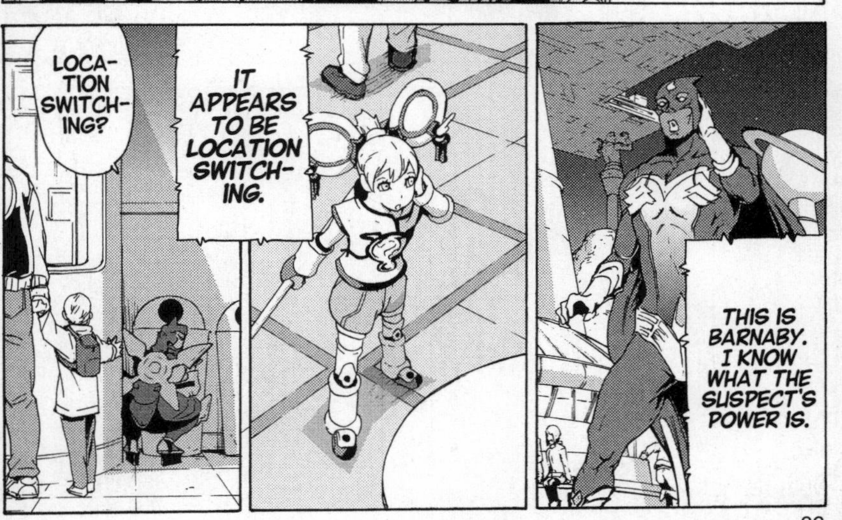
AGNES...
WHAT IS IT, BARNABY?
I'D LIKE TO ASK A FAVOR.
?
UGH...
BARNABY HAS A MESSAGE FOR EVERYONE. I'M OPENING UP THE LINE.
HUH?
THIS IS BARNABY. I KNOW WHAT THE SUSPECT'S POWER IS.
IT APPEARS TO BE LOCATION SWITCHING.
LOCATION SWITCHING?

HE CAN SWITCH PLACES WITH ANOTHER PERSON.
KRNCH
SO THAT'S HOW!
I'D LIKE TO ASK EVERYONE TO DO SOMETHING.
NO WAY!
WHY WOULD I...
WHSH
POOOSH
TAK
...DO WHAT YOU SAY?!
PSSSH

FWOOSH
TOMP
HYAH!

YAAAH!
GWAAWAWHAM
WHAM
EEK!
OOPS! SORRY!
WHY'D YOU DO THAT?!
BUT I THOUGHT ...!

HA HA HA HA!
SHWRRRRR
SPIN
HUH?
POOF
THUD
AGH!
POOF
MOMMY!
POOF
POOF

HA HA HA HA!

AS HEROES, WE MUST PROTECT THE PEOPLE.
...

ATTENTION, GUESTS OF THE PARK!

A FUGITIVE HAS ENTERED THE PREMISES. PLEASE FOLLOW STAFF INSTRUC-TIONS TO EVACUATE.

I'M SURPRISED TO HEAR YOU CARE ABOUT THE PEOPLE.

AND I'VE GOT JUST THE PLAN!

NO.

FIRST, I'LL GO
POW!
AND THEN...
THAT'S MY PLAN!
WHAMMO!
I DON'T GET IT.
IT'S ABOUT VIGOR!
I DON'T EXPECT ANYTHING FROM A PLAN BASED ON GUTS!

HEY! THIS IS NO TIME FOR ARGUING!
WHAM
WE JUST GOT WORD FROM THE JUSTICE BUREAU.
■ROBIN BAXTER
THE SUSPECT'S NAME IS ROBIN BAXTER. HE'S A DANGEROUS THIEF KNOWN WORLDWIDE.
THERE ARE REPORTS OF THEFTS IN MULTIPLE COUN-TRIES.
BUT HE HAS NEVER BEEN ARRESTED. HE ALWAYS ESCAPES.

THE HEROES ARE ASKING THE CITIZENS TO EVACUATE.

WE PAID MONEY TO GET IN HERE!
WHAT'S GOING ON?!
HURRY UP AND CATCH THAT THIEF!

SURE THING, DAD!

POOF !

THERE HE IS!
SWSH
GYAH!

ZIP
EEK!
URGH!
FWUF
EEK!
TOMP
ARE YOU OKAY?!
WHSH
YES...
THAT JERK!
POOF
POOF
POOF

EVERY-ONE, LISTEN UP!

TIGER & BUNNY
THE MOVIE
The Beginning

SHWR
SHWOOSH
WHSH

WHOA!

HM?!
SHWRR

DID YOU PREFER LI'L BUNNY?

WHSH

TUP

HAH!
FWSSH
?!
SKIDD

LOOKING FOR ME?

!

HUP

LET'S FINISH THIS!

I'M BURNING TOO MANY CALORIES!

HEH...

YOU CAN'T RUN ANY-MORE.
POLICE

YOU GUYS ARE IDIOTS!
FWAAASH
KCHIK
WHO'RE YOU...
FOOSH
...CALLING AN IDIOT?!
TNK

SWUP
WHAM
GRAB
WHAT?!

GO ON! GO AHEAD AND SWITCH!
IT DOESN'T MATTER WHICH ONE OF US YOU SWITCH WITH...
...SO DO IT!
GLANCE
...

HEY!
WHSH

YOU GUYS REALLY ARE IDIOTS!

YOU'RE NOT GOING TO SWITCH?
HUH?!
SIGH

LIVE
TIGER AND BARNABY! SHOWING OFF YOUR TIGHT FRIENDSHIP WON'T CATCH THE CRIMINAL!

WOULD YOU LET GO OF ME?
OH...!
FWAP
WHAT KIND OF PLAN WAS THAT?
I THOUGHT HE WOULD SWITCH WITH ONE OF US, SO...
DID YOU REALLY THINK HE WOULD FALL FOR SUCH A SIMPLE TRICK?!

AT THIS RATE, THE VIEWERS WILL CHANGE THE CHANNEL.
HMPH
COME ON, MAN...
...OUR MAIN JOB ISN'T GETTING ON TV!
WHAT-EVER.

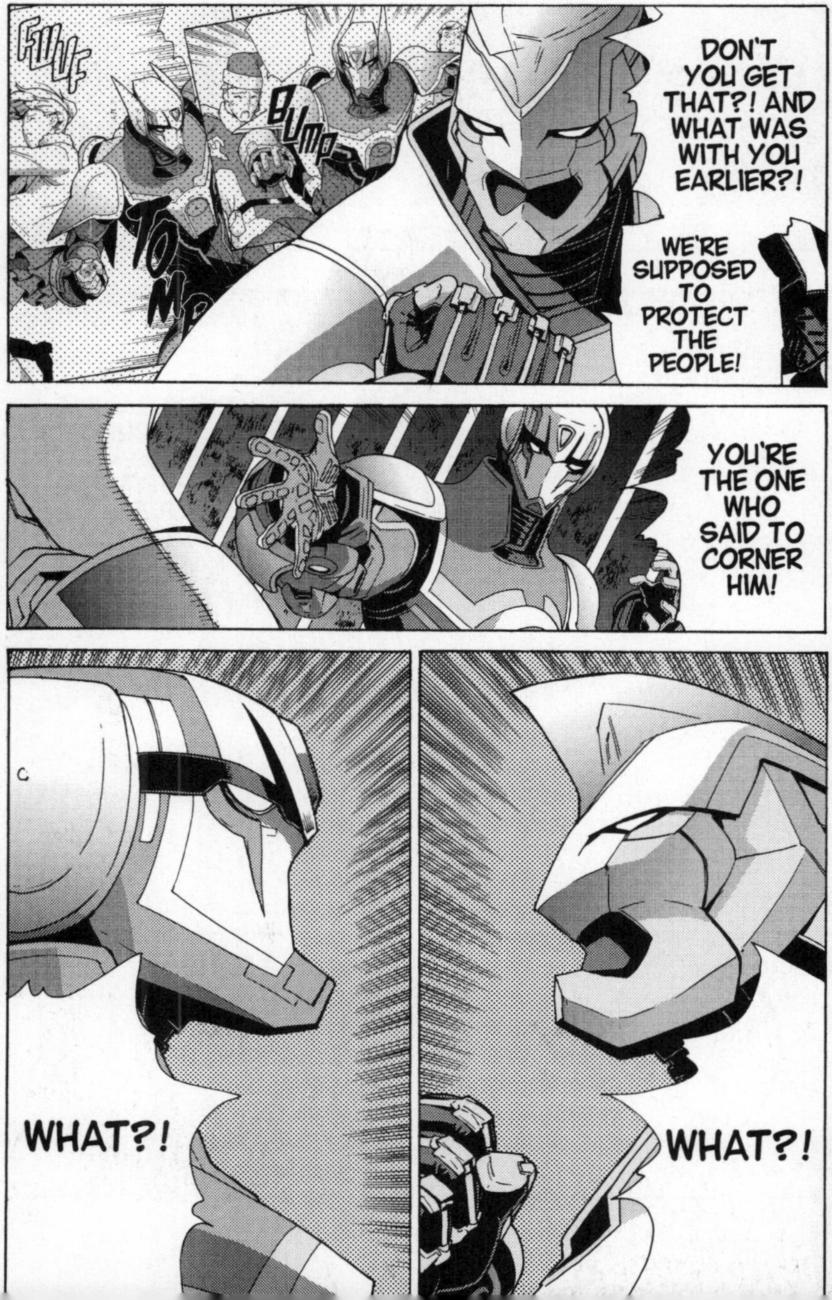

DON'T YOU GET THAT?! AND WHAT WAS WITH YOU EARLIER?!
WE'RE SUPPOSED TO PROTECT THE PEOPLE!
BUMP
TOMP

YOU'RE THE ONE WHO SAID TO CORNER HIM!

WHAT?!

WHAT?!

ROBIN BAXTER, WORLD-RENOWNED CRIMINAL, IS PROVING TO BE QUITE A HANDFUL FOR OUR HEROES!!

BIG TREE

GWOOSH

FWUPPP

THE HEROES ARE NOW SEALING THE PARK TO BLOCK ANY ESCAPE ROUTE.

THEY ARE ALSO EVACUATING THE PEOPLE.

FWUF
UH-OH!! WE CAN'T GET CLOSE EITHER!

THIS AREA IS
CURRENTLY
CLOSED OFF!
PLEASE FOLLOW
INSTRUCTIONS
AND GATHER AT
THE GATE!

BIG TREE

!!
NO ONE MOVE!
!

SMIRK
THAT CREEP!
GET OVER HERE!
WHOA!
YANK

HURRY! OVER HERE!
NOW EVERYONE STAY STILL!
WHAT? WHAT? WHAT'S GOING ON?
YOU'RE SO DUMB!
WE'VE SEALED OFF THE AREA.
AND?
IF EVERYONE IS GATHERED HERE, HE CAN'T SWITCH WITH ANYONE TO GET OUT.

HEH... SO THEY'RE NOT ALL STUPID.

NOW WE MUST THINK OF A WAY TO CATCH HIM, MR. WILD!
WOW, YOU GUYS ARE SMART!

HOW LONG DO WE HAVE TO PUT UP WITH THIS?
...

WHSH

COME BACK!
SMIRK
SLIP
WHAH ?!
POOF
!

THANK YOU!

HELLLP!

!!
SHWRR

I'M GOING AFTER THE SUSPECT.
WELL, YOU'RE ON YOUR OWN.
I'M GONNA GO HELP HIM!

IT'S HIS OWN FAULT FOR RUNNING OFF!
ARGH!

DAAAD!
!
DAD!
STAY WHERE YOU ARE!
AGH!
SLIP

WE WILL ALWAYS PROTECT YOU.
GROW UP TO BE A KIND PERSON WHO PROTECTS OTHERS.

OKAY!

HUH?
ZWSH

SHOOM
HUUUH ?!

FWSH

DAD!

OH!
SIR...
...PLEASE STAY WITH YOUR SON.

YOU'RE THE ONLY FATHER HE'S GOT, AND YOU MEAN A LOT TO HIM.

DO YOU LIKE KIDS?
WHAT?
YOU DID THAT FOR THE CHILD.
AND EARLIER TODAY...

IT'S JUST...
...UN-EXPECTED.

...
I DIDN'T DO IT FOR ANY PAR-TICULAR REASON.
...
BIG TREE
NOW THEN!

THE HEROES ARE HEADING FOR THE ROLLER COASTER WHERE ROBIN HAS FLED!

NORMALLY, THEY HAVE A COMPLETE ADVANTAGE, BUT NOT THIS TIME!

COAST

STOP

STOP

STOP

THIS STALEMATE MIGHT CONTINUE FOR A WHILE!

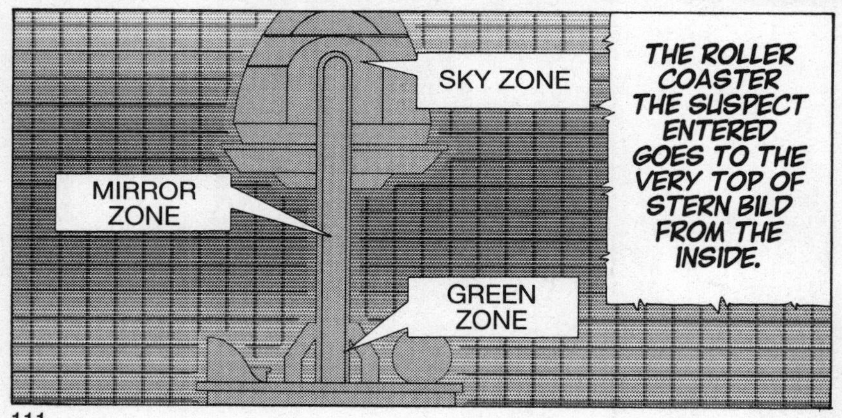

THE TUNNELS PASS THROUGH THE GREEN ZONE, MIRROR ZONE AND SKY ZONE.
THE EMERGENCY EXITS ALONG THE WAY ARE LOCKED...
...BUT THE SKY ZONE EXITS ONTO THE OBSERVATORY OVERLOOKING THE WHOLE CITY.
IF THE SUSPECT MAKES IT THERE...

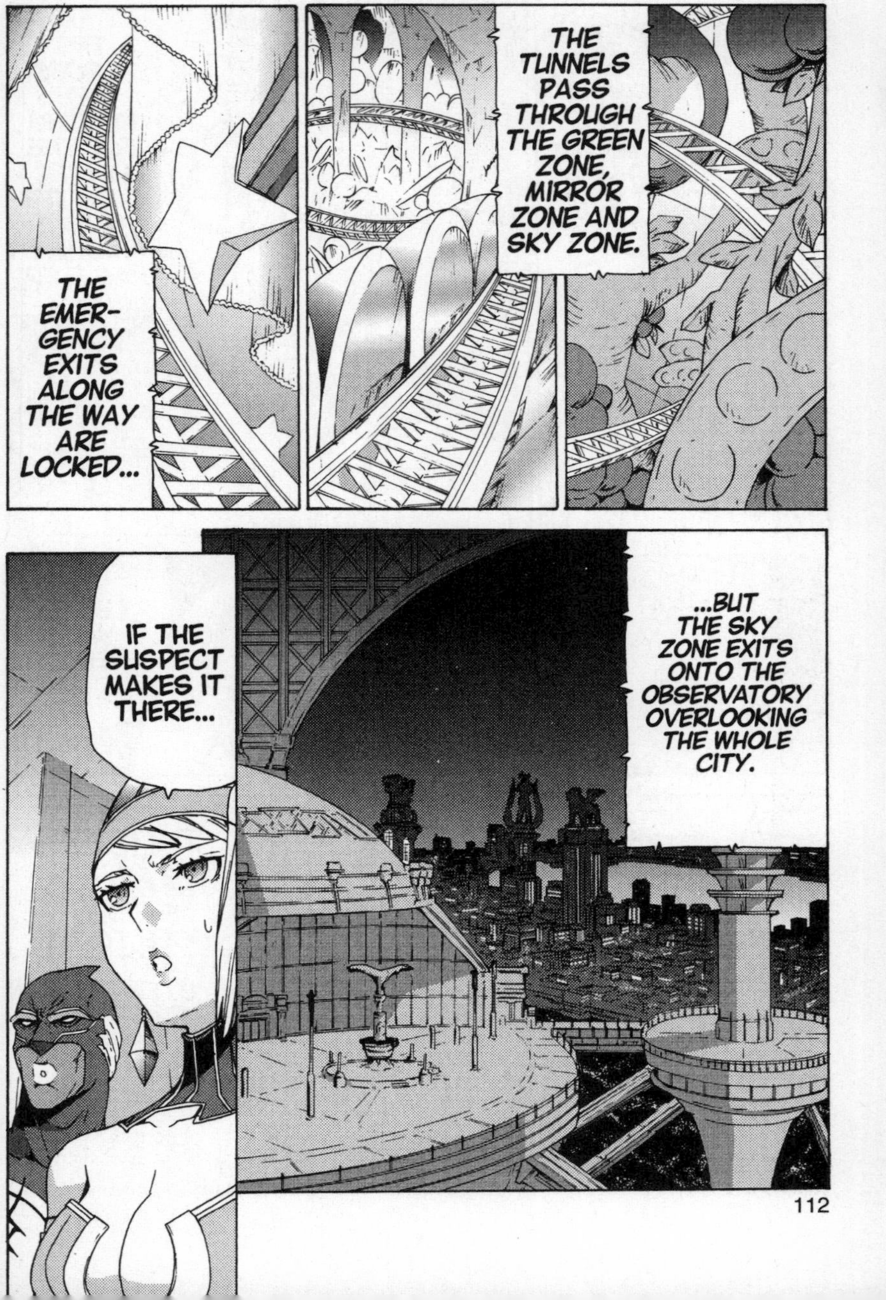

HE WILL BE ABLE TO SWITCH WITH ANYONE IN THE CITY.

YOU HAVE TO CATCH HIM BEFORE HE REACHES THE OBSERVATORY.

OH, NO...

HE MUST NOT GET AWAY WITH THE STATUE OF JUSTICE.

BUT HE CAN SWITCH WITH ANYONE!

WHY NOT DESTROY THE WHOLE BUILDING?

THE FINES WOULD BE HORRENDOUS...

WHAT A NASTY OPPONENT!

GAAAH!

ROBIN HAS PASSED THE GREEN ZONE AND ENTERED THE MIRROR ZONE!
!!!
!

WHAT?! AL-READY?!
DON'T RUSH ME! I'M THINKING!
GAH! THIS IS GETTING NO-WHERE!

WHAT?! I WAS GONNA BE A DECOY FOR YOU!

THAT'S IT!

WHAT? WHAT IS IT?

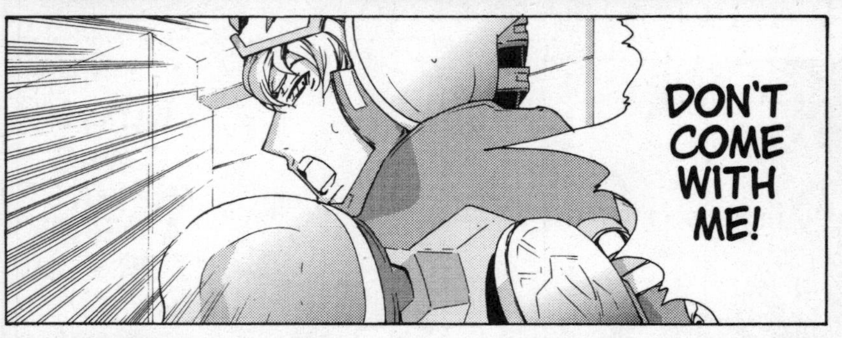

I'LL CATCH THE SUSPECT MYSELF!

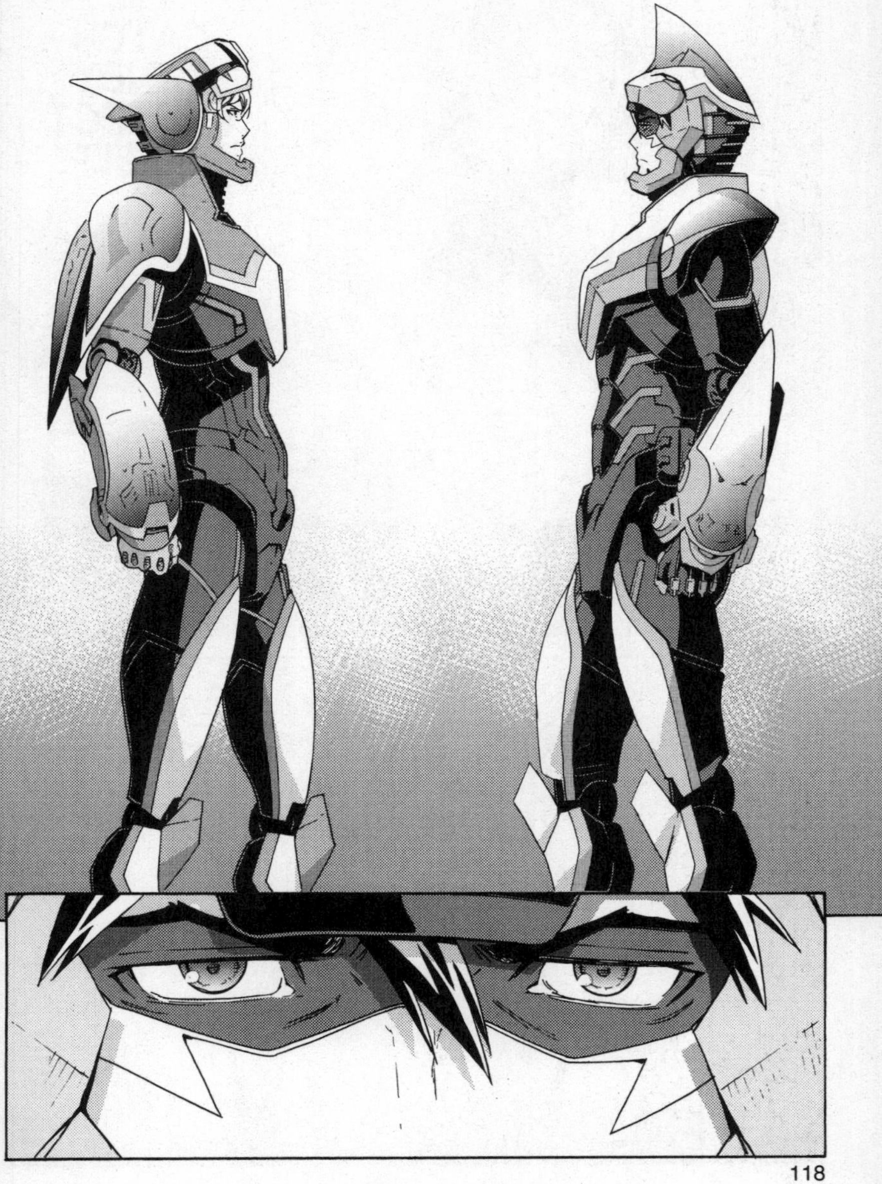

KLANG

WHSH

HUP

HEY, IS IT OKAY TO LET THE NEW GUY GO OFF ON HIS OWN LIKE THAT?

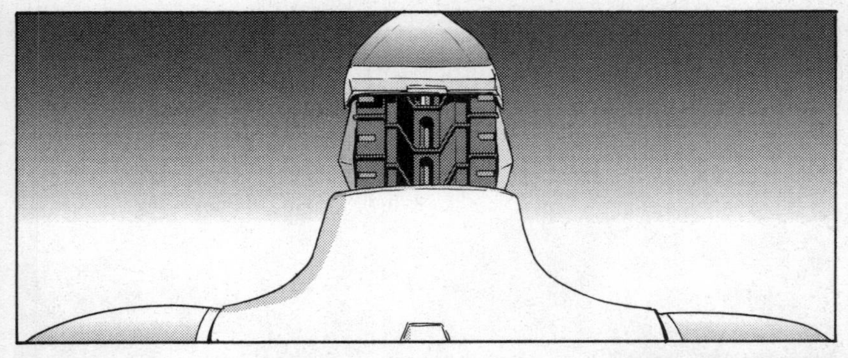

SCREECH
MMM!
MMM!

ROBIN BAXTER IS ALMOST PAST THE MIRROR ZONE!

WHSH
HWSH
SHWRRR
?!

...

THE SUSPECT HAS ALMOST REACHED THE OBSERVA-TORY!
...

WHAT IS BARNABY DOING?!

YOU'VE REALLY CAUSED A LOT OF TROUBLE!
!

BUT THE GAME'S UP! WE'VE GOT YOU!

YOUR STUPID DUO IS SURE TO FAIL!!

SHWRR

!

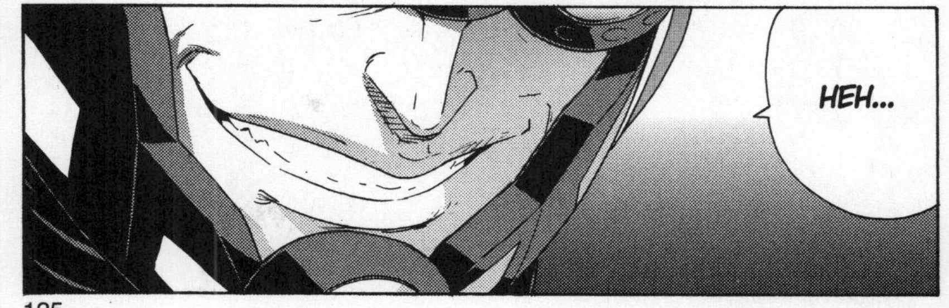
HEH...

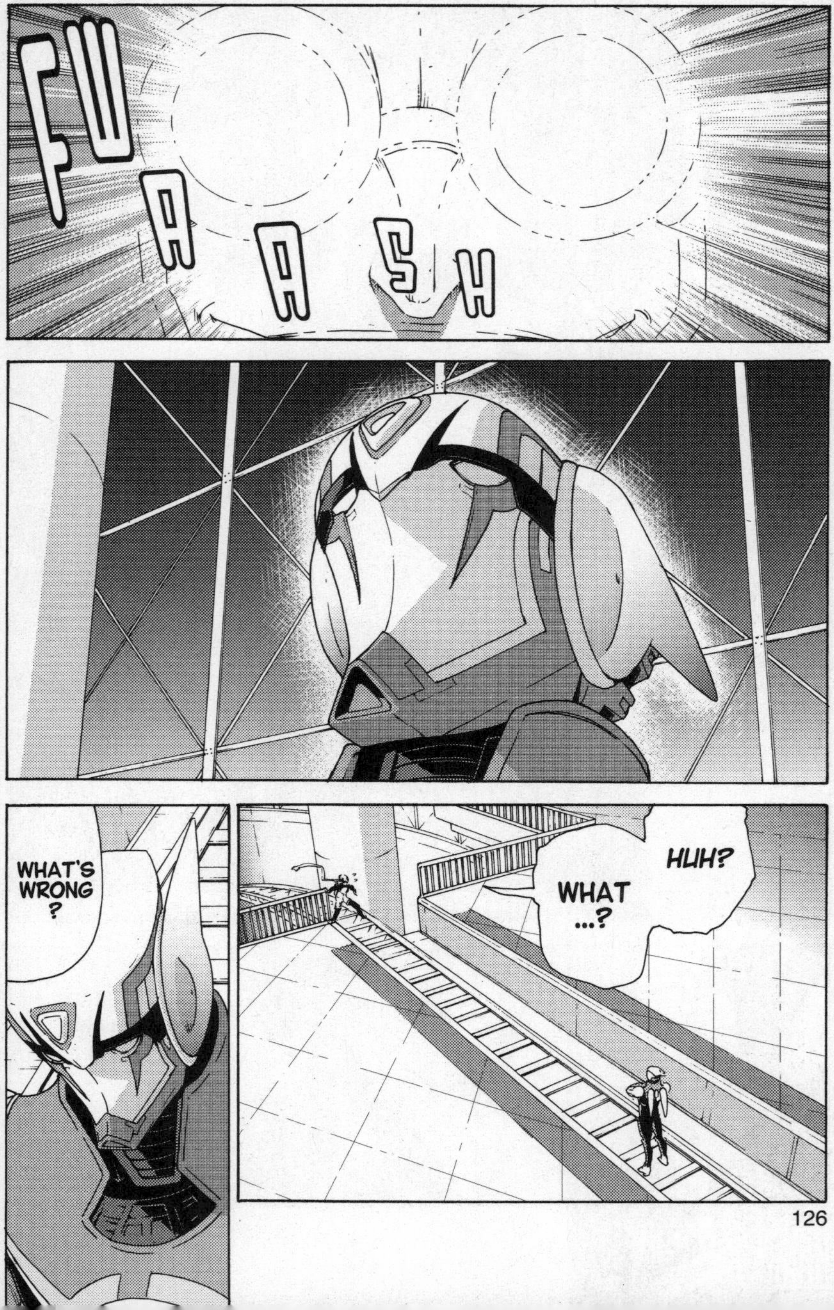

FWAASH

HUH?

WHAT ...?

WHAT'S WRONG ?

ARGH!

HUP

00:00:29
THIRTY SECONDS TO POWER DEPLETION.
GAH!
!!

WHSH
HAAH!

CLANG
BONG
CLANG

CLUNK
CLONK
ARGH! I CAN'T SEE ANYTHING!

KANG
HMPH!
GYAIEEE!
RINNNNG
BAM
BAM BAM

IT'S OVER.
00:00:00
I'VE CAPTURED ROBIN BAXTER.

WHUP
WHUP
WHUP

IT'S OVER! THE ROOKIE HERO...

...BARNABY BROOKS JR. HAS CAPTURED ROBIN BAXTER...

...AND SUCCESS-FULLY RECOVERED STERN BILD'S STATUE OF JUSTICE!

HERO'S BAR

NOT BAD!

THAT WAS EXCIT-ING!
THE RATINGS ARE THROUGH THE ROOF!

GOOD! WE'LL DO A SPECIAL ON BARNABY! AN UP CLOSE AND PERSONAL DOCU-MENTARY!

...

IS THAT THE BEST YOU CAN DO?

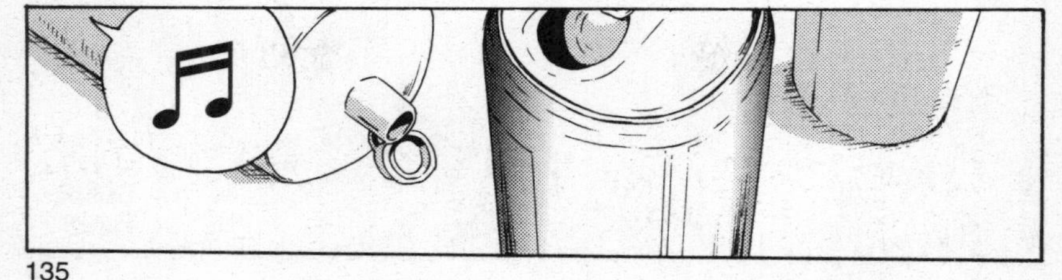

CON-GRATS.
YOU DID GREAT, LI'L BUNNY.

STOP CALLING ME THAT!
OH, STILL BEING A SOUR-PUSS?

LET BYGONES BE BYGONES!

DON'T TALK TO ME THAT WAY!

KACHAK
GOOD WORK TODAY.

OH...
THANK YOU.

IT WAS A LENGTHY STRUG-GLE!

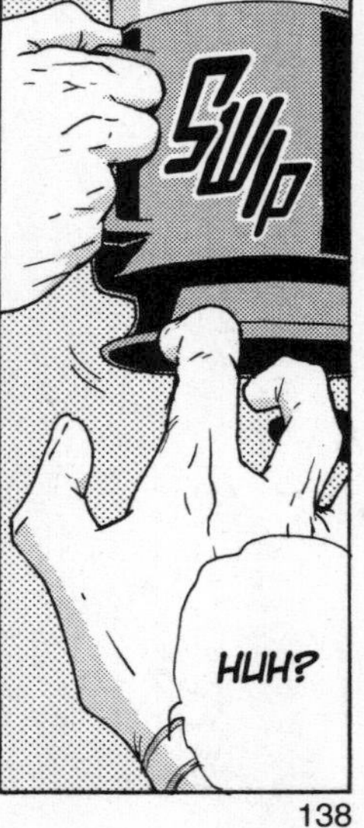
SWIP
HUH?

I WASN'T CONGRATU-LATING YOU. YOU DIDN'T DO SQUAT TODAY!

YOU WERE MAGNIFI-CENT.
YES, I DID!
KEEP UP THE GOOD WORK.
YES, SIR.

...

I'M SORRY, KAEDE!
I WAS SO SCARED!

IF DADDY HAD BEEN THERE, HE WOULD HAVE PROTECTED YOU!
I WAS FINE WITHOUT YOU, DAD.

THERE'S A NEW HERO CALLED BARNABY. HE SAVED ME!
HUH?
HE'S REALLY COOL! I'M A FAN!
ALL RIGHT. I'LL MAKE THE SUIT EASIER TO REMOVE.
THANK YOU.
I'M SURPRISED YOU THOUGHT OF REMOVING THE SUIT.
IT JUST CAME TO ME.
STILL...
...YOU TWO ARE A STRANGE TEAM.
HUH?

I SAW THE FOOTAGE RECORDED BY YOUR SUITS.
WILD TIGER
Barna
WHAT ARE YOU TALKING ABOUT?
I HAVE TO SAY ...
...YOU SUR-PRISED ME YESTER-DAY.
...

I'LL CATCH THE SUSPECT MYSELF!
ARE YOU GONNA LET THAT ROOKIE CALL THE SHOTS?
I DON'T HAVE TO DO WHAT HE SAYS!
WE CAN'T LET HANDSOME GET ALL THE CREDIT!

WAIT!
UM...
I WASTED THREE MINUTES OF HIS LIFE, SO...
WHAT ARE YOU TALKING ABOUT?
I DON'T GET YOUR POINT!

TIME!
DO YOU HAVE SOME BASIS FOR PUTTING YOUR TRUST IN HANDSOME?
NO TIME AT ALL.
YES, I DO!
I HAV ...
...A GUT INSTINCT!
HUH?!

HIS PERSONALITY MAY BE A LITTLE...NO, VERY UNPLEASANT...
UM UM
...BUT HE'S DOING HIS BEST TO CATCH THE CRIMINAL!
AS HIS PARTNER, I'LL WATCH OVER HIM!
I'LL TAKE RESPONSIBILITY IF ANYTHING HAPPENS!
SO PLEASE...
CHK
...LEAVE THIS TO HIM!
HRAH!
WHSH

HMPH!
KANG
IT'S OVER.
I'VE CAPTURED ROBIN BAXTER.

HEH...
HON-ESTLY, I WAS KINDA NERVOUS.

I SAID I'D TAKE RESPONSI-BILITY, BUT I COULDN'T DO ANYTHING.
...

HA HA HA HA!
BUT HE CAUGHT THE CRIMINAL. YOU'VE GOT AN EYE FOR TALENT!

OH MAN...
TRMBL TRMBL

WHAM
WHUD
BZZZT
BAM
WHOA! THAT WAS CLOSE!

TALK ABOUT UNNECES-SARY...

CLAP CLAP
CLAP CLAP

I DIDN'T GET TO SING ON CAMERA ...
...AND I BROKE A NAIL!

I WAS SO IRRITATED AFTER-WARD THAT I COULDN'T SLEEP!
I PIGGED OUT ON ICE CREAM ALL NIGHT!
WHY ARE YOU BLAMING ME?

HE WAS POPULAR AT THE HERO ACADEMY.
HE TOTALLY STOLE THE SPOTLIGHT. HE MAY BE HANDSOME, BUT HE WON'T BE POPULAR UNLESS HE'S ALSO A NICE GUY.
IT'S YOUR PARTNER'S FAULT!

I ACTUALLY DON'T KNOW MUCH ABOUT HIM.
HE WAS ...
ZIP
...SO POPULAR...
ZIP
...THAT HE HAD...
ZIP
...A FAN CLUB.
ZIP

WHY ME?!
YOU KNOW HOW YESTERDAY'S WELCOMING PARTY FELL THOUGH?
WELL, TONIGHT WILD TIGER WILL TREAT!

SO LET'S ALL GO DRINKING TONIGHT!
UGH!
GRB
WHAT?!?

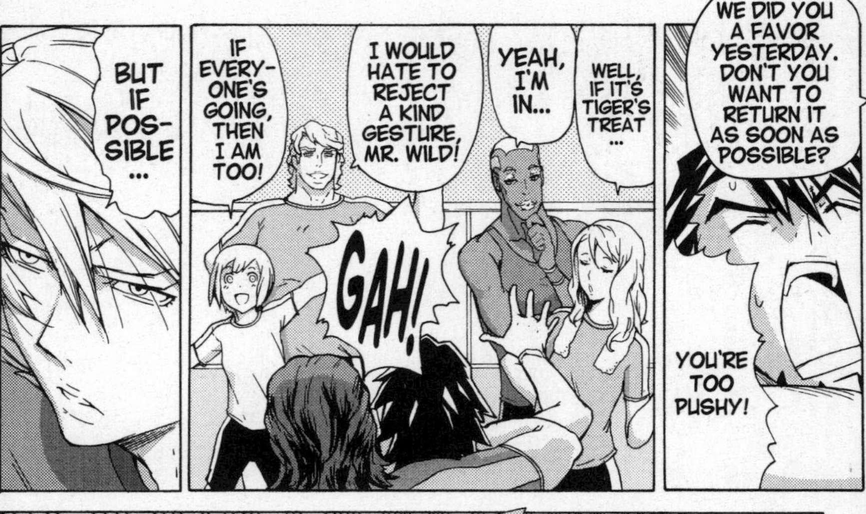
WE DID YOU A FAVOR YESTERDAY. DON'T YOU WANT TO RETURN IT AS SOON AS POSSIBLE?
YOU'RE TOO PUSHY!
WELL, IF IT'S TIGER'S TREAT ...
YEAH, I'M IN...
I WOULD HATE TO REJECT A KIND GESTURE, MR. WILD!
IF EVERY-ONE'S GOING, THEN I AM TOO!
GAH!
BUT IF POS-SIBLE ...

...I PREFER A RESTAU-RANT THAT SERVES MISO SOUP!
ZWIP

HMM... GORILLA!

...

OH WELL...

TOMOE...

I GUESS I'LL TRY TO MAKE IT WORK WITH HIM.

FATHER... MOTHER...

AND ONE OF THESE DAYS, I'LL FIND OUT THE TRUTH.

!

KOTETSU T.KABURAGI

HELLO?

TIGER & BUNNY: The Beginning

Side B

VIZ Media Edition

Art by **TSUTOMU OONO**
Planning/Story **SUNRISE**
Original Script **MASAFUMI NISHIDA**
Original Character and Hero Design **MASAKAZU KATSURA**

First published in Japan in 2013 by KADOKAWA SHOTEN Co.,Ltd.,Tokyo.
English translation rights arranged with KADOKAWA SHOTEN Co.,Ltd.,Tokyo.

Translation & English Adaptation **LABAAMEN & JOHN WERRY, HC LANGUAGE SOLUTIONS**
Touch-up Art & Lettering **STEPHEN DUTRO**
Design **FAWN LAU**
Editor **MIKE MONTESA**

Printed in the U.S.A.

Published by VIZ Media, LLC
P.O. Box 77010
San Francisco, CA 94107

10 9 8 7 6 5 4 3 2 1
First printing, October 2013

RATED T FOR TEEN

PARENTAL ADVISORY
TIGER & BUNNY: THE BEGINNING is rated T for Teen and is recommended for ages 13 and up.
ratings.viz.com

www.viz.com

STOP!

YOU'RE READING IN THE WRONG DIRECTION!

This is the END of the graphic novel

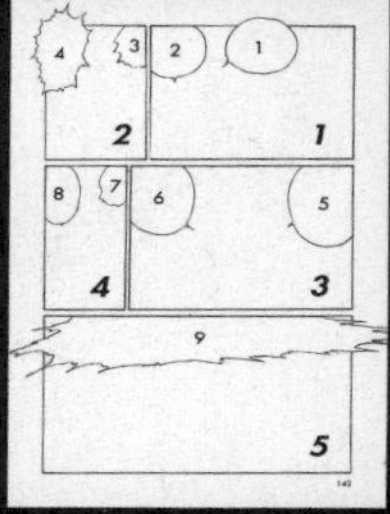

To properly enjoy this VIZ graphic novel, please turn it around and begin reading from **RIGHT to LEFT**. Unlike English, Japanese is read right to left, so Japanese comics are read in reverse order from the way English comics are typically read.

This book has been printed in the original Japanese format in order to preserve the orientation of the original artwork. Have fun with it!

⇦ Follow the action this way.